Vulnerability
The Art of Letting Go

Lauren J.

Cover designed by The Joyous Marketing Team
Editing and Formatting by Self-Publishing Services

Printed in the United States of America

First Printing: January 2021

ISBN- 978-1-7331182-3-1

The Rollercoaster of Vulnerability

ACKNOWLEDGMENTS

To the ladies of James 1:4, this rollercoaster ride would have been meaningless without you. Thank you, Angela, Jocelyn, and Chelsie for holding on until the END. Nydia, thank you for coming along and becoming the SHIFT we needed. We are now Jeremiah 1:5. To be continued…

OTHER BOOKS BY THE AUTHOR

Purposeful Pain Volume I

Lauren shares her personal journey through a pain that began in childhood and culminated in a devastating divorce in adulthood. In these darkest moments, she caught a glimpse of God's will and found the purpose in her pain.
Available on Amazon.

Purposeful Pain Volume II
Prayer Journal

The Purposeful Pain Prayer Journal is a companion piece to the inspirational book Purposeful Pain. Each chapter coincides with a chapter in Purposeful Pain. Scriptures lead into space to record your own journey through life's challenging moments.
Available on Amazon.

Intimacy: A Twist of Faith

Lauren G. Jackson lays bare the path to intimacy from the perspective of both partners in this book. Each chapter in this fast read marks the progress in their relationship with each other and their understanding of God's purpose for them as individuals and together.
Available on Amazon.

FOREWORD

As a new day dawned, ushering in Friday, March 13, 1987, I lay awake with tiptoe anticipation. This was the day that my life would change forever! This was the day that I would join the ranks of all the women in the world who wear the title of "Mother". Yes, this Friday the 13th a C-section delivery was scheduled to be performed, and a beautiful gift would be bestowed upon me and her father in the person of Lauren Nichole Grimes (Jackson).

Having suffered a pelvic fracture as a result of a fall from a fig tree (one of the vagaries of living on a farm) in my tender years, the end thereof was cephalo-pelvic disproportion. This condition would not allow a fetus to make the normal trek down the birth canal. I should have known that in as much as I would not experience a normal delivery as I had hoped, this baby would not be one who would gravitate toward the status quo, business as usual, or all things basic. She would be a trailblazer, a forerunner, a midwife who would help others birth purpose, and would, in Harriet Tubman-like fashion, allow others to mount a freedom train whose port of call is wholeness through purposeful brokenness.

The treatise that you are getting ready to embark upon will unveil the most essential element needed in your quest for wholeness. Vulnerability is truly an art, dear readers. It requires laying bare your imperfections, idiosyncrasies, innermost thoughts and all the things that make you who you are. Once you are comfortable with the divulging process, the laying aside of the weights that keep you bound and incapable of experiencing true freedom will be easier to achieve. This is not to suggest that vulnerability does not have its price. Lauren will share with you the intricate details of how she ascended safely upon the mountaintop, having mastered the art of letting go, by way of the valley of real-life experiences.

Divorce was the catalyst which fueled her need for wholeness. Having had a front row seat to the vagaries of divorce as a young teen, Lauren witnessed brokenness personified in me. She witnessed a mother whose life was torn in pieces and left with a gaping wound. What she did not witness was the healing process that would lend itself to complete restoration and wholeness. As you delve into this most powerful read, you will discover her determination to HEAL! She will give you some do's and don'ts if true liberation is to ultimately be realized.

You may wonder what qualified her to tender her thoughts on the subject of "Vulnerability: The Art of Letting Go". Well, dear readers, I humbly submit to you that experience is in fact the best teacher. In as much as life is replete with ebbs and flows (highs and lows), mountaintop experiences and valley days, my precious, God-fearing daughter, has drunk deeply from the fountain of them all. But here's a bit of good news that the Apostle Paul impressed upon the Corinthians, and all of us, by way of extension: "Now thanks be to God, who always leads us in triumph in Christ, and reveals through us the sweet aroma of His knowledge in every place" (2 Cor. 2:14 WEB). Testimonies are borne out of tests. What you are about to witness through this book is a testament to the goodness of God amid adversity!

Having been afforded the opportunity to co-author, proofread, and sit with her first book and best seller, *Purposeful Pain*, and now *Vulnerability: The Art of Letting Go*, I witnessed the evolution of a baby girl who swam through an ocean of dysfunctionality, became a wife and mother (in that order), "experienced" what she "witnessed" (divorce), and came out better for it! Need I say, you are in for the ride of your life! Embrace it; there's purpose in it!

Gleefully submitted,

Patsy J. Jones

Minister of the Gospel

Certified Life/Career Coach

Heart2Heart Coaching, LLC

ONE: THE BIG CHOP

Have you ever found yourself asking God for what you thought you were ready for? Perhaps you had become obsessed with your future and where you were headed because you'd come out of a cycle of pain; you'd gone through the process of purposeful pain, and now you're ready to get out into the world and really show it of what you're made.

So many times, I've been ecstatic about where I was headed, having prayed that God would give me the desires of my heart. When He came through for me, I became afraid, not knowing what to do with what God had bestowed upon me. On my journey toward wholeness, I have deduced that letting go and letting God have full reign in my life is truly an art.

Once you have mastered the art of putting all things in the able keeping of God our Father, you will have arrived at a place called vulnerability. I will be the first to admit that vulnerability is a terrifying concept. Giving life to it can be all the more frightening. You will find in this book my journey of vulnerability, including the true art of letting go and allowing the perfect will of God that you've been fasting and praying for to be made manifest in your life, and how truly awesome it is.

In that process, we find "the big chop."

If you've ever dealt with trees, shrubs, or even houseplants, you can attest to the fact that pruning or cutting away dead limbs or leaves ushered in new life. Women who have natural hair know that when they made the decision to go natural, it was necessary that they experience the big chop. They had to cut away all the relaxed areas of their hair and start fresh to gain the look they desired. In this life, God often has to do the big chop in order to remove the people, places, and things that have led us to believe that what we are is normal, when the truth is, all that we are is abnormal, at best.

When you are facing the big chop, you are facing the scariest moment of your life by far. Imagine standing on a cliff overlooking a beautiful city, beholding a beautiful landscape and preparing to jump with nothing to keep you safe but a bungee cord. With God as your bungee cord, you're not going to hit rock bottom because He's not going to let you. But the ability to let go and free fall, to trust that taking the jump will not be to your detriment, is the ultimate in vulnerability. The big chop in this scenario mirrors the cutting away of the very things that hinder a total surrender of your will and way to your omnipotent God. When you come to the end of yourself, you discover that God was there all the time.

Additionally, the big chop requires becoming real with who you are. You must look in the mirror at what you said you were versus what you can handle becoming. And those two things, when they meet, can be very scary. How easy is it to go through life complaining and putting off on others the ugly issues you carry? But if you ever get smart enough to look at yourself, you would learn that acquiring the ability to take inventory of yourself is truly the first step toward becoming vulnerable.

LAUREN J.

The first person that you must become vulnerable with when you are learning how to release and open up to others is the man or woman in the mirror. And that's very scary because now the pressure is on you. You take the responsibility away from the other person—the other party to the event—and you focus on yourself. Self-reflection: what did I do? What did I control—or not?

In the big chop, you'll find that you must lay aside all of that baggage: the hurt that you've gone through, the pain, the lies you've told yourself about yourself. Do you recognize these? "I'll never be happy." "Oh, God is not going to send me the mate who I desire." "I'll never have the job or the career." Or, even worse, "I'll never have the purpose that I desire. I'll never feel purposeful."

Many people don't feel purposeful, so coming to the realization that perhaps, "I've been my own stumbling block," is an uphill battle. Maybe you only condemned yourself because it was too hard to believe that good things could happen to you. Perhaps you had gotten so used to having bad things happen to you, you built a wall around yourself, decreasing your expectations and settling for the pennies that you were accustomed to receiving in this life. Because you've done that to yourself, anything that shows that life, indeed, could be better, you see as a threat, not an opportunity.

You must view it as an opportunity, not a threat. In essence, you have been given the golden opportunity to look at yourself and embrace the big chop. Chopping off old relationships, chopping off places you used to frequent, and chopping off old wardrobes you used to parade around in—all suggest that everything you do outwardly is nothing more than a reflection of what's going on inwardly. So, when you have to do the big chop, you must chop outwardly (publicly). That means you have to be open to people seeing your change.

How scary is it for you when people see you morph into a new creation? Very. People are so fickle, and they can use words to enslave you and enclose you in areas where you don't belong—holding you hostage by your past. Your change makes them uncomfortable because they see it as a condemnation of themselves, and they aren't ready to change.

The big chop is so beautiful, especially when you cut away all those things that you've hidden behind. All the contrivances you claimed you embraced, because you wanted to become what the world would peg as the ideal you, were all for naught. What man *thinks* about you is of little importance, but what God *knows* about you is paramount. First Samuel 16:8 encourages us: "The Lord does not see as man sees; for man looks at the outward appearance, but the Lord looks at the heart." In truth, you avoided the big chop in an effort to conceal the fact that you really were not a roaring tiger, but more like a defenseless kitten. If the world knew the tender branch who is the real you, how would they deal with you? Would they mishandle you? Because you were not comfortable in your own skin for fear of being judged, you felt compelled to continuously change your stripes: change the way you look, the way you dress, the way you talk, or who you hung out with. Wouldn't it have been much easier to come to the resolve that God, in His infinite wisdom, thought enough of each of you to make you *individuals*? Yes, dear readers, all of you were "fearfully and wonderfully made..." (Ps. 139:14).

In this book, prayerfully, you will realize the necessity of coming to grips with who you are inside, who that little boy or that little girl is inside. Because by doing that, not only will you meet *you* for the first time—and it's going to be absolutely beautiful—but you will allow the world to meet you unapologetically. You'll allow the world to meet the best version of you, and you won't care what the world thinks because you will have found all that you were hoping for in yourself.

I challenge you in this season—chop it all off. You're

about to go from struggle to strength as you make your way through each chapter. Get ready; it's going to be a wild ride!

"...LET US LAY ASIDE EVERY WEIGHT, AND THE SIN WHICH SO EASILY ENSNARES US, AND LET US RUN WITH ENDURANCE THE RACE THAT IS SET BEFORE US, LOOKING UNTO JESUS, THE AUTHOR AND FINISHER OF OUR FAITH..."

~HEB. 12:1B-2 (NKJV)

TWO: LIVING NAKED

Now you have to learn how to allow yourself to live naked. What I mean by living naked is living openly with your truths, your successes, your failures, and your secrets. (You share the latter with a select few who you are sure would never judge you.) Living naked is so scary, especially when you've been through so much pain. Of course, you've gone through the steps toward wholeness and have gotten to the point where you feel like, "Okay, I'm letting go of all of the things over which I have no control," but the truth is, you secretly haven't. You still have walls up. And so, when the person comes along who wants to love you naked, you put your walls up all over again. You almost turn around and walk away because you question how they could possibly want to love those areas of your life, and to love you like that?

Face it. A certain level of trust must be established before someone is allowed to love you naked. Fear sets in, coupled with the worry that the flaw you reveal could cause them to run away and never come back. Convinced that their response will be negative, you are hesitant to share with them. Sometimes you take the opposite approach; you want to share the worst things about yourself with the hope that they will just end the process. In your mind, this behavior is validated by the fact that all of the others have left, so there's no point in revealing your true self or approaching the process with strength and confidence.

If you don't ever bother being transparent, or you don't approach it in a way that gives the other person room to respond with compassion, you don't have to deal with your own flawed nakedness—the real person behind the mask. And that, too, is just another wall. You have to learn how to balance both. Balance being naked with being open to love.

I can attest to the fact that being naked and open to love can be terrifying. You want to throw up both your hands and say, "I don't want to deal with that." I will subject a potential mate to the greatest scrutiny, searching for that thing that will justify my retreating based on my own desire to remain concealed. I don't want to live that open, that free.

After having gone through purposeful pain, during this stage of my life where I'm rebuilding and cautiously dating, I'm on a quest to figure out what I really want. Outside of being the wife, the mother, the career woman, at my very core, what do I want? I'll be honest; I thought I knew.

After my divorce, I had this five-year plan, all mapped out, and it did not include a mate. It only included my desires. And now, I'm being challenged to visit it all over again.

For so long, I thought I had it all figured out. In retrospect, my ex-husband and I were married for ten years. We had our financial strategy for building wealth, and we had our routine of what to do in the fall, spring, and summer. I didn't need to think about any of this. But now, after the pain, I'm having to contemplate my entire future, and I'm frustrated because I don't feel like dealing with this again, having to chart my own course. Most especially, I'm having to learn to live naked.

Rest assured, dear readers, I know where you are in the

realm of living naked because I've had to share some of my pain with others, and that's scary. I've had to address sensitive questions, like why, at thirty-one, I can't have any more children. Nothing was wrong with me medically, but I went through both of my pregnancies being beautiful yet being treated like crap. I experienced the vagaries of both verbal and emotional abuse. This fueled my decision to never get pregnant for another man because he would mishandle me and then leave me to do all of this child-rearing by myself. I did what I felt needed to be done. Having a tubal was the result of brokenness and self-protection. As providence would have it, this really great guy comes along and he has no kids and I'm thinking, "Oh God, look at what I did! Why would you want me?"

But let me encourage you; it's not what you did in the midst of being shattered but what you do moving forward. What God has for you is for you. You can't run away from what God has strategically planned for your life or scare it off. The person for you will treasure you in your nakedness, with your scars and blemishes, your stretch marks, and your selfishness, and will love you past it. It truly happens, but you've got to be okay with coming out from behind what you've been clothed with and living naked, on purpose. It's the only way. My dears, get ready to unclothe yourselves and allow people to accept you there, unapologetically naked.

"NOTHING IN ALL CREATION IS HIDDEN FROM GOD'S SIGHT. EVERYTHING IS UNCOVERED AND LAID BARE BEFORE THE EYES OF HIM TO WHOM WE MUST GIVE ACCOUNT."

~HEB. 4:13 (NIV)

THREE: WHAT'S KEEPING YOU?

Very recently, I had to really contemplate what's keeping me from embracing the uncomfortable, so that I could become unstoppable. And what I realized was that fear was the culprit that kept me from propelling myself forward. I'm certain that I am not alone in this struggle. Most people are so afraid to risk it all and chance reaching greater success, they will forfeit hope for the future to remain in their comfortable state.

You'll find yourself staying in relationships that you know, first and foremost, don't have the quality of soil to grow the seed that God has deposited within you. As a result, you become angry, upset, disappointed, and downright unhappy because you're in a soil that won't allow you to grow. You don't say, "Let me go hop into the soil that I know will produce a favorable harvest," having seen evidence that this soil can truly propel you forward. You would much rather become complacent in the wrong soil, even, sometimes, be planted in the wrong season. Because you've been there so long, you come to believe that's where you were meant to be.

Complacency is the enemy's trick. The enemy's job is to convince you to settle for the status quo. Let me give you some Word right here: "Therefore, if any man be in Christ, he is a new creature: old things are passed away; behold all things are become new" (2 Cor. 5:17 KJV).

That scripture describes evolution. You were all born as infants, but did you remain as infants? No, you didn't. As a matter of fact, through your maturation process, more of your years are adult years as opposed to infant's years. Your time in the ground as a seed, so to speak, is much less than your time of bearing fruit.

A fruit's characteristics are indicative of the soil in which it was planted. Consider this: The fruit that comes out, which is your adulthood, is nothing more than a reflection of the soil in which the seed has undergone the germination process. A seed does not remain a seed longer than a tree remains a tree. A seed does not remain a seed longer than an apple becomes an apple. Once an apple becomes an apple, it is an apple for life. Once a seed is planted in good soil, it becomes a fruit. Seeds are designed to yield fruit, always evolving or morphing.

I've never seen a seed become another seed, so why would you be content to keep your mind in a state of complacency? That was never God's design for you. A seed goes through a process once placed in soil. In that soil, it deals with rain. In that soil, it deals with sunlight. In that soil, it deals with fertilizer. All of this is for it to become what its ultimate design is.

Don't forget that in the germination process, the seed must die in order to yield fruit. In like manner, the outward man must perish so that the inner man can be renewed day by day. God's design for evolution is an upward movement. The more water, sun, and fertilizer you encounter, the more beautiful you are.

That's what makes your pain so purposeful. That's what makes your brokenness so beautiful. That's what makes your ashes so great. None of what you've gone through during the maturation process was designed to define you; it was to put you in a position such that you would live and not die. You could become what you were supposed to become and live forever. Not for the moment. And not only would you live forever, but you would bring wholeness to the person who dares to bite into you. As women, we like to be the apple of our man's eye. Why? Because I want to be the substance that you bite into that transforms your digestive system. That changes everything internally about you.

So, what are you really connected to? What's keeping you?

I cannot abide relationships where people are together because of the fear of paying child support. Man, you are constantly entertaining her, trying to be nice, and pacifying her with fifty dollars here and one-hundred dollars there. You don't want to be obligated by law to pay her $500 a month. You don't realize that the fifty and the one-hundred dollars you keep giving her on the side, plus the cost of entertaining her, is placing what you were designed to become in bondage. That's nothing but the enemy's trick. If the enemy can convince you that you can't afford not to be nice to her, then he can constantly imprison you and he doesn't have to place you behind physical bars.

You'll end up depressed, broken, and lonely because you are not producing the fruit that God ordained. All the while, you're seeing others who are flourishing and you can't step out of your situation to be a part of that. Fear keeps telling you: if you do this, then they'll do that.

VULNERABILITY

So many relationships end up on life support because each person is afraid to pull the plug. I'm just pinpointing one example. I'm sure you know of many other ways relationships can be dysfunctional.

I had to ask myself why I kept falling into relationships where I was the stronger vessel. I *was* the stronger vessel. I came in and put a process in motion that changed someone else's whole dynamic. You could have called me a narcissist because I wanted to feel like a savior. I wanted to feel the enjoyment of being the one who changed how someone else looked at life.

That was not supposed to be. I was supposed to be the woman whose whole dynamic changed because of the man in my life. And together our two powers, being in sync, would impact the world.

But that could never come to fruition because I was in bondage to the fear of what would happen if my expectations were unrealistic, at best. I had to stop looking **at** what I was looking **for**! What if he wasn't as fine a man as I was used to? What if he's not making the six figures that I was used to? Should that be tantamount in building a healthy relationship?

Let's keep this in mind: what I was used to didn't help bear the fruit that God had planned for my life. It gave me the process, right? It gave me fertilizer, sun, and water. It gave me the cycle of germination, but it wasn't what I was designed to be.

What I had to understand was that every man who came to touch me could not contain me. He didn't have the soil that was needed to grow me into what the next level looked like for me. He couldn't take me from an apple to applesauce and change my characteristics.

I'm now at a point where I'm in search of someone who can change my entire countenance. Change my stinky thinking, my negativity, my view of myself, my way of

LAUREN J.

speaking to myself, my way of speaking of others. I want him to be the one who makes me level up because I am so used to being the one who levels up others.

But I had to go through a process, and in this season of going through, I am longing for the uncomfortable. The stuff that makes me take three hours to find one outfit because I don't want to be too this or not enough of that. I'm understanding that this soil is different from any soil I've encountered heretofore.

I implore you, readers, to figure out what's keeping you. Is settling for safe more appealing than reaching for the uncomfortable? Which one will yield more fruit? Is it you sitting where you've always been, saying, "This is all I was meant to be," or you standing out in the crowd, saying, "God, I want my will to be lost in your perfect will for my life. I want you to empty me of me so that you can fill me with you?"

I want to die empty for God, so that whatever was keeping me can't keep me anymore. Even the grave couldn't keep Jesus. It held him temporarily until His resurrection. When the women came to the sepulcher where he was buried, only to find Him gone, they then believed that He was who He professed to be. He didn't have to say it anymore. He didn't have to keep reminding them that He was a prize and all they needed. God didn't need to have an ego because His actions portrayed who He was. The seed that He was, was to yield the fruit of eternal life. Yes, His seed was the fruit of life. So I ask you, what's your seed? What soil are you in? What's keeping you?

*"IF THE SON THEREFORE SHALL MAKE YOU
FREE, YE SHALL BE FREE INDEED."*

~ JOHN 8:36 (KJV)

13

FOUR: MOVING TOWARD
THE UNCOMFORTABLE

When you've been hurt so many times, when life has failed you and you've even failed yourself, it seems nearly impossible to wrap your mind around, "What if, this time, things don't fall apart?" Life can condition you to believe that what you are is all you will ever be. You procrastinate when you really should be fighting like hell to move close to the uncomfortable. You are aware of what comfortable feels like because you've sat in it long enough. However, as frightening as it might be, life is a journey that is replete with ups as well as downs, and you must maneuver through them all.

Yes, the act of becoming sedentary, sitting under life's shade tree, can be to your detriment. You've complained about how your so-called "happy place" ceases to bring you any comfort, when the truth of the matter is, you're really unhappy. The question is, are you unhappy enough to embrace the uncomfortable? Are you ready to move from stagnation (stuck in the now) to destination (that place of purpose)?

In this chapter, I am going to dive deep. There will be a lot of personal moments here, so hold on tight as you and I wade through uncharted waters. Let me begin by saying, I believe there are moments when you allow people to become your distractions with their problems and issues, lending to your inability to focus on yourself and your own self-healing. All too often, you find it much easier to see the scars on your brothers and sisters than to look in the mirror and discover your own and ultimately deal with them. Yes, you may be able to look at your scars, but do you really feel them? Can you still feel those deep lacerations? Have you felt the healing process as a result of these cuts and bruises? I submit to you that it is important that you feel those moments.

Everyone wants to be strong. It's not a compliment to anyone when you tell them, "Oh, you're so weak!" Being weak is looked upon as taboo, as something that is low and despised; it makes you turn aside from vulnerability, when truly you are your strongest when you are your weakest.

Here's a word from the Lord in that vein: "*And he said unto me, 'My grace is sufficient for thee: for my strength is made perfect in weakness.' Most gladly therefore will I rather glory in my infirmities, that the power of Christ may rest upon me*" (2 Cor. 12:9 KJV).

In that moment of what the world may call weakness, you are able to be your most authentic self. Nothing is more beautiful than when you are able to be completely open and walk in your truth, whether it is representative of weakness or strength. That place is scary for most people; I admit it is scary for me.

I am definitely guilty of focusing on others and pouring myself into them in such a way that it enables me to hide the things I'm feeling. You see, I am a servicer. I love to service. I love to give, and I love to help people reach their goals—so much so that I neglect to focus on my own goals and aspirations. I love to buy into someone else's dreams. When I'm in a relationship, my focus many times is solely on that person, their dreams, and what they want to do, instead of them being a complement to my life.

As I am embarking on this new life at thirty-one, and being single and out in this dating world after ten years of marriage, it is important to me that I take time to be both a service provider and a self-servicer. At this juncture, I am healing. And healing is a process not of time but of action. People can be working on something for years, but if that work proves to be nonproductive, it should not be looked upon as having been all for naught. Tunneling through a situation that did not reach your expected end has a way of teaching you how to approach future endeavors. I confess that I've been guilty of spinning my wheels, focusing on others and on being the perfect person in their lives, all the while failing to be the perfect person to me.

My moving toward the uncomfortable is allowing myself to be alone. I have never been alone. I've been in a relationship off and on since high school. Now, I am divorced from the man who I was with since I was seventeen; that's fourteen years. No, I've never been alone with myself to really connect with whom I am at my core.

Know this as you're reading this chapter: everyone's process of moving toward the uncomfortable will look different. For some of you, it will be getting into that relationship with a corny person whom you otherwise would not give the time of day. Perhaps it will be leaving your broken relationship that does not have the proper soil to fertilize your seed. You may be in a position where you are stepping out of your comfort zone and opening up to the person whom you're with, and that gives you pause. Uncomfortable is different for everybody. I'm just sharing with you what it looks like for me.

As I'm embracing this moment of letting go of the things and people that distract me—not entertaining the vagaries of others, not being hasty in jumping on board with this one or that one—but really taking time to truly connect with myself, I am wanting to learn what I believe I deserve. What do I tell myself about myself? What broken areas in my life are critical and must be fixed so that I will never go back into the same cycle that I left? Most importantly, what is it that I believe about myself that has allowed me to let someone mishandle the treasure that I am?

The Apostle Paul, when writing to the Corinthians in 2 Cor. 4:7, asserts: *"But we have this treasure in earthen vessels, that the excellence of the power may be of God and not of us."* This is to suggest that the Lord shines brightest through those who have been broken, and who have given themselves, as a result, to His use.

As I have yielded myself to the uncomfortable call from God to be a conduit through which His word might flow, I have come to understand that the treasure of the gospel is in fact contained within the frail, fragile, and fickle bodies of all the redeemed. And when you, as Christians, allow yourselves to be vessels prepared for service, it is then that God's glory will shine through your humanity, and it will be readily recognized as His power, not yours.

In this season, I endeavor and I implore you, dear readers, to allow God to lead you through the valley of the uncomfortable that will ultimately lead you to your destiny in Him. Yes, it can be scary, especially being vulnerable with yourself. Thinking something and saying it out loud are two totally different things. If something is just in your head, and you haven't verbalized it from your lips to God's ears, you don't think that it's real. Once you start speaking it over yourself and you allow those words to get out into the atmosphere where you cannot go back and return them to your mouth, or back into your head, it becomes real.

My dears, I further implore you to be vulnerable with yourself, first and foremost, before ever trying to be vulnerable in your relationships, your friendships, or your marriages. Start with you and give yourself the safety net that you need to be your most authentic self. That bears repeating: give yourself the safety net that you need to be your most authentic self! In that moment, you truly get to define and see who you really are. And how can you ever explain to your significant other what you need, if you have not discovered or defined what that need is?

Your need can only be revealed when you take the time to do self-service. Moving toward the uncomfortable forces you to dig deep inside yourself. It lends itself to moments of reflection and isolation. Dear readers, it is important that you tell people who are in your life, "Hey, honey, if I am distant, it is not you; it's me self-servicing me!"

Remember, you can't be your most authentic self in a relationship that requires effective communication if you have not taken the time to really learn and master the art of "you." Get your PhD in yourself before you try to get it in someone else. Focusing on others will only distract you from seeing your own brokenness. The perils of not seeing your own brokenness are that the jagged edges of your life will begin to cut on the person to whom you're closest.

The prophet Isaiah is a prime example of the importance of moving toward the uncomfortable and seeing yourself for who you really are. In Isaiah Chapter 6:1-5, this prophet had a vision that served to reveal his own sinfulness. He saw himself as a man of unclean lips whose sinfulness disqualified him from joining the seraphim (meaning "burning ones," those angelic beings who dwell so close to the presence of God that they burn with holy brilliance) in praise. Isaiah truly saw himself as he was allowed to experience God's majesty, and that ultimately led to his repentance, forgiveness, and commission to carry out God's work.

How could Isaiah even call others to repentance without first recognizing his own flaws and then experiencing God's forgiveness personally? Here is Isaiah's story according to the scripture: *"In the year that King Uzziah died, I saw the Lord sitting on a throne, high and lifted up, and the train of His robe filled the temple...So I said: 'Woe is me, for I am undone! Because I am a man of unclean lips, and I dwell in the midst of a people of unclean lips; for my eyes have seen the King, the Lord of hosts'"* (Isaiah 6:1,5 NKJV).

I share this scriptural passage with you as an

admonishment that sometimes there are Uzziah's in our lives who must die so we can see clearly the things we must crucify within ourselves. An uncomfortable and careful examination of myself may shockingly reveal that, in fact, I have issues and my issues have issues!

> "BUT LET EACH ONE EXAMINE HIS OWN
> WORK, AND THEN HE WILL HAVE REJOICING
> IN HIMSELF ALONE, AND NOT IN ANOTHER.
> FOR EACH ONE SHALL BEAR HIS OWN
> LOAD."
>
> ~ GAL. 6:4-5 (NKJV)

FIVE: WHAT DO I DESERVE?

When your whole life has been plagued with a multiplicity of bad and dysfunctional occurrences, you are forced to ask if you were deserving of the hand that you were dealt. I am just coming out of a divorce, and I find myself pondering that very thing and wondering how the contemplation of what I deserve translates into wholeness. Furthermore, how do I break the daunting cycles in my life to ensure that my children will not have to live out the generational curses that I have had to endure? My quest for understanding what I deserve is borne out of hurt and of my desire to heal those wounds that were part of that hurt.

At this juncture, people who have come in and out of my life have been mere reminders of my own brokenness. It is so scary because I'm working so hard to collect the fragments of my broken heart and present them to God, the ultimate potter, whose desire is to put me back together again. I struggle every day not to be that same girl who was once shattered by the storms of life and a failed marriage. I don't want to go through a repeat of history. In this season of my life, I aspire to experience real, true love, not only for myself but for my boys as well. The sad reality is that our Black boys are already growing up in an environment where they are being preyed upon as opposed to being prayed on. Many of them are being abused and tossed aside; they are seldom reminded of how much they are loved. They come out of the womb and into the world in a state of brokenness. Truthfully, I've got two sons whom I don't want to groom in brokenness. Understanding what I deserve will be of utmost importance when trying to display self-worth to them. This has to be one of the hardest things, knowing what you deserve and forging ahead with a plan to get ahold of it.

Growing up, I spent so much of my time wanting my father's approval. That desire equated to me graduating as a junior from high school, matriculating through college and getting a degree, and not returning home as an unwed mother. Instead, I endeavored to join the workforce and chart my own course. As a matter of fact, I never returned home to live under my mother's wings. I moved away, got married, had a promising career, and waited several years to plan our first child. I did everything I thought would make me successful in my father's eyes. In retrospect, my quest to please him became an obsession that I brought into my marriage. I wanted to be accepted; I wanted the good job and the pat on the back more than anything. Because of this unhealthy fixation, I took on more than I should have taken, signing up for a brokenness through which I had already lived. My brokenness was a place of comfort for me. I knew it all too well.

Now back in the dating arena, when the nice guy comes along who wants to get to know me, is willing to carve out time to spend with me, and who is intrigued by me, I don't know how to accept it. So far, I've met two guys who are really nice, and I have trouble with them. I feel like, "Oh, they're too nice." They don't get my attention at all. But the guy who's critical of me, who is emotionally unavailable, who is broken within himself—oh, I'm just a magnet for that persona. In fact, that is where my heart lies, with those who are in need. It may be because, in so many ways, I've mirrored the damsel in distress, the one in need. I don't know how to let a man, a real man, come into my life and be to me all those things I desire. I'd rather a broken man transform into a whole man, transform into the man I believe I need, to heal me. That has got to be the craziest thing ever. That toxic thinking defies all logic.

There exists a dichotomy in the way that sometimes I know my worth and what I deserve, but, at the same time, I don't see myself as being worthy of it. Consequently, it becomes easy to settle for the comfort of brokenness because that's something I am acquainted with.

Dear readers, if you can relate to this way of thinking, then you are probably convinced that you know how to cure brokenness. You know what medicine to take for it, and it's comforting for you. The tragedy is when you don't transcend into something better and you find yourself hurting perpetually. You've become attached to a shattered life, and you're disappointed. But why? Why are you disappointed when you signed up for that same brokenness?

As I'm speaking to you on the subject of brokenness, incrementally inching my way toward wholeness, I want you to feel these emotions and realize that the struggle is real. I am a person who is really going through this. And it's so scary for me because with every fiber of my being, I want the nice guy, but at the same time, I don't believe that I deserve his love. I've spent so many years of my life in a dysfunctional relationship, and I see the same evolve among family members, so I've never seen a healthy relationship up close. I don't even know what the identifying traits are, what it looks like. And when someone tries to save me and bring me into the light of a healthy relationship, I am clueless about to how to handle it. I feel that I'm in a place outside of my normal habitat.

Consequently, my heart bleeds because I want the

opportunity to enjoy a healthy relationship. I want my boys to experience real love and not transactional love that says, "If you do this for me, then I love you." I want them to experience and see it, so they can model it for the world. My sons are my two contributions to society, to the Black male species. Using common vernacular, I don't want to "jack them up" with the dysfunctions that I've seen.

How do I fix it? How do I decide what it is that I deserve? Perhaps I must settle on the biblical assertion that I am "...fearfully and wonderfully made" (Psalm 139:14). I believe that many of you reading this, or listening to it, are probably wondering the same thing. How do we get there? Stay tuned. I guess we'll figure it out. Merely being cognizant of the areas of brokenness in our lives is a milestone toward reparation.

"On that day tell your sons, 'I do this because of what the Lord did for me when I came out of Egypt.'"

~Exodus 13:8 (NIV)

SIX: SYNTHETIC VS. THE REAL PEACE

I always wondered how would I know when I found real peace. In retrospect, much of my life has been spent in synthetic peace. Synthetic peace affords a high for a moment, and in that moment, everything is good. You feel like you're experiencing real peace, but it's simply an illusion that is temporary at best.

Peace is something that sticks with you no matter what happens during the course of your day. You can still be at peace, come what may. Something may disrupt a moment, but it will not disrupt your peace. Ultimately, you are in control of your own state of being. You never allow people to have "remote control," turning your emotions on and off, and sending you out of control or into a state of unrest. When I became cognizant of the fact that people could easily remote control me, I discovered that what I embraced was not real peace but momentary satisfaction. In the realm of synthetic peace, a moment would live up to the expectations I created for it, rather than me finding the joy in the moment regardless of its imperfections. Synthetic, simply put, means fake. I had to understand that fake peace can mimic the real thing for a moment, but that's it. It's fleeting at best.

Peace in its purest form is when your world may be turned upside down and you are buffeted by the vagaries of life, but it doesn't concern you. You are not affected emotionally by what it looks like—whether the bills are not getting paid on time, or you are being pulled in many different directions simultaneously. In the midst of it all, you still feel the comfort. It is in that moment that the peace of God, which really surpasses all understanding, can be realized. As a result, you are able to operate at a level of excellence you have never before achieved. Notwithstanding the chaos that may loom large in your life, you still have joy that the world didn't give and cannot take away.

I'm reminded of and can identify with what the Apostle Paul said in Philippians 4:11, *"I am not saying this because I am in need, for I have learned to be content whatever the circumstances."* The beauty of this contentment is that it is not contingent upon whom you are dating, or who is in your life romantically. That is the realest peace you'll ever encounter; it's not being remotely controlled by someone else who is being flagrant about being so "into you" when they really are not. They love you, but they don't even know you; they barely know your full name.

Peace that is genuine can only come supernaturally. Jesus has this to say in John 14:27: *"Peace I leave with you; my peace I give you. I do not give to you as the world gives. Do not let your hearts be troubled and do not be afraid." (NIV)* If you ever want to experience real peace, I implore you to encounter a calm in the midst of a storm while holding on to God's unchanging hand. Rest assured that He is going to work all things out for the good of those who love Him. There is no need to get frustrated or try to make something happen. God is the author and finisher of our faith, and He will speak all things into existence according to our faith and perfect those things concerning us. When your mind is clear, your heart is pure, and your temple is clean (not infiltrated with the toxic things of this world), you can experience the joy and peace that is yours for the taking.

Truly, dear readers, I am happy with Jesus alone. My greatest fulfillment comes from the impact I have on others as I engage them with the heart of God. Peace will overtake you when you're not masking hidden agendas, and trying to make more money so that you can purchase frivolous things that bring no glory to God. Such things only afford momentary satisfaction. When your resolve is, "God, I just want your will do be done," when you surrender to Him and allow your will and desires to be lost in His, you are afforded so much peace. He will elevate you to places that you've never even dreamed of and give you the love that you never thought you could have.

That is where I sit in this season. I am at such peace at this juncture in my life. When God does decide to send my soul mate, he won't be encountering a person who is being remotely controlled by the universe, but one who is in control, directing who she is at all times. It is so gratifying when someone enjoys being in your world. They are not constantly concerned about choosing their words, so as not to easily offend or set you off. They see you in control and not governed by a remote control. You are representative of a safe place where someone can be their authentic self. It is the most rewarding thing ever to have a peace that truly transcends all understanding. A peace that is out of this world!

I implore you, dear readers, to be in search of real, true, genuine peace that only comes from God, and let the synthetic stuff go because it will only serve to leave you empty after you have apprehended it.

"NOW MAY THE LORD OF PEACE HIMSELF
GIVE YOU PEACE AT ALL TIMES AND IN
EVERY WAY."

~ 2 THESSALONIANS 3:16 (NIV)

SEVEN: SEEING ME THROUGH THE EYES OF ANOTHER

*T*he first time I saw you, I only saw a person. Nothing in particular stood out. Nothing in particular really resonated with me, but the second time I saw you, I saw me for the first time. It was one of the most out-of-body experiences I ever had. The woman who stood before you was a broken, scarred woman, who did not know her own beauty. I knew that I was gifted, but had yet to tap into my God-given purpose. Being left over and picked over so many times had begun to affect my self-confidence, but that came to a screeching halt when I saw myself in your eyes.

I walked through the double doors carrying a scar that he did not know about as he sat there. Previously, when I had been longing for validation, I was met with the reminder that rang often in my ears, "Stop asking if you're pretty. I'll tell you when you're not." As this phrase rang in my ears over and over, I wondered if I even looked presentable. Then I walked into the room, and, as I did, his smile came beaming at me. He was breathtaking, strong, and he could own a room. But what made him stand out in the crowd was that you could see his humility with every greeting and hug that he gave to others who shared the same room as me.

He worked the room, speaking with and making sure everyone was having a great time. In that moment, my eyes were fixed on him, and I do not recall if I was still breathing! As I walked across the room, our eyes met, and as I tried to look away quickly, he caught me in mid gaze. I looked down, trying not to blush, telling myself I was hoping that he was looking at someone behind me, but in my heart, I was hoping that was not the case. To my surprise, he walked toward me, speaking to those around me in a gentle voice as he made his way to me. The first thing he said was, "I didn't recognize you. You look beautiful, darling." It was almost as if this was the first time I had ever received a compliment, which I can assure you is not the case.

Honestly, I never saw me until that moment. It was almost as if he had hoisted me out of a pit of pain and cleaned me off, sat me in front of a mirror and said, "Look! Look at this! Who do you see?" As we gazed into each other's eyes, it was as if he was reading my heart, searching for the insecurities I was hiding behind. I quickly came to myself and my face grew hot as I tried to respond in a way that would not scare him off. I replied softly, "Well, thank you, sir", and as the evening went on, we exchanged more pleasantries. I admired him from across the room, as he admired me as well. When the night ended, he walked me to my car and before I could get inside, he pulled me into his muscular arms for a goodbye hug, and I immediately thought of Whitney Houston. Whitney starred in one of my favorite movies, "Waiting to Exhale" and, in that moment, I felt like I was replaying my favorite scene. I closed my eyes, as I inhaled and exhaled, taking in his cologne and scent. I was in the arms of a man, and not only was I made to feel safe, but I was able to feel the relief of vulnerability. After embracing, he looked in my eyes and gave me a forehead kiss that literally sent chills through my body. He gave me his card, which included his cell phone number, and said I needed to let him know when I had made it home safely. I was speechless; the entire evening was more than I had ever anticipated! On my drive home, I replayed all the pleasantries we had shared from that night, knowing that I would hold on to them forever.

Sometimes, when you have gone through so much, you are not whole and it's hard to see who you are. As women this certainly rings true. The sad reality is that many times you really don't know who you are until you see yourself in the eyes of a person who admires you—until you see yourself in the eyes of a person who sees your future self as greater than your current circumstances.

In that moment, something he said snapped me out of the trance I had been in for years. Yes, for years I sat in a trance of brokenness. I had no clue that I was still beautiful to the outside world. To me, I was just okay and just existing. Never did I believe that I was above the stars, or that I deserved more than what I had settled for in my past. And it wasn't just in his tone; it was in his eyes. When he looked at me, it was as if he was looking into my soul. He saw my scar, and instead of pointing out the presence of the scar, he created an environment where my scar no longer existed. In that moment, he was my comforter. But he had no clue what I had faced and what I had endured. He had no clue that I did not know who I was.

Actually, I always had a way about me. I carried myself in a high-caliber fashion, always exuding confidence, when in fact I was not confident at all. But it was not until I saw me in his eyes that I knew that something about me was different. In fact, I was unusual, not in a weird way but in a way that made me believe that I was powerful and beautiful. I believe the Apostle Paul, who explains it in 2 Corinthians 4:7, "But we have this treasure in earthen vessels, that the excellency of the power may be of God, and not of us" (KJV), had *me* in mind. That scripture suggests to me that not only do I house the treasure (presence of the Holy Spirit in my life), but I, too, am a treasure who is to be treasured. His look assured me that I was still desirable, and all of the things that I had lost were not in vain. It was almost as if he saw me wearing my brokenness as a cloak and was eager to rid me of it. His look reminded me that I didn't need the cloak because brokenness was no longer a part of my story.

Unlike most men, he complimented my character, reminding me that I was strong, smart, courageous, and innovative, and that I could never be boxed. Never will I forget the moment wherein he exclaimed, "Lauren, sometimes you have to strike out before you're able to come back and hit a homerun." I did not understand what he meant then, but I get it now. He knew that I was a winner, even when I did not. He always knew that I was destined for greatness, even when I didn't know I had a purpose. I thought that my life was supposed to be spent working, making a lot of money, taking care of my sons, and traveling and doing things that made me happy. After this encounter, I began the quest to live for more than just myself. After seeing me in his eyes, I accepted that God was calling me for greater, for more. I didn't know what it would cost or how long it would take. I had no clue how hard it would be, but I knew that there was something more on the other side for me, more than that to which I had been exposed. The things I had been exposed to were surface things, but God was trying to give me something eternal: my purpose.

And so I began to take this leap of faith and learn to live vulnerably. I no longer desired to rob those around me of the experience of loving the most authentic version of myself. What made this encounter so special for me was that in this particular season, I was at a low space in my life. Consequently, his ability to speak so gently to my brokenness truly made all the difference. My beauty stood out to him because it was what drew him to me, but it wasn't what stabilized him. It wasn't what mesmerized him. It was his ability to see my heart pumping through my chest, displaying the overflow of love and comfort that only a man in search of a soulful woman could see. He knew what he was looking for, and he knew when he saw me that he had found it. But he also knew that I did not know. He knew that in order for me to be prepared to even be in his world, I would have to be crushed beyond measure, crushed beyond where I was to be dissolved by him. Most importantly, he cared enough to give me the grace and space to evolve.

So here I am, once a grape and now a wine after being crushed. Having taken losses and learned hard lessons, I was once broken. But now I'm whole. I see clearly now what he saw all along. He saw a woman on fire, a trailblazer, an example for others to follow. Ultimately, he saw me as a model for the world, not only for myself or my children. I would be a mother for the nation of women, breaking generational curses that I didn't even know I could influence. Yes, he knew when he saw me that all of that was in me, but he waited patiently until I saw it in myself. I thank God every day for his eyes, for I never saw me until I saw me in him.

Dear readers, I tender this chapter as an ode to a God-sent angel with eyes like mirrors, designed for me to see my value in!

"BUT LET PATIENCE HAVE HER PERFECT WORK, THAT YE MAY BE PERFECT AND ENTIRE, WANTING NOTHING."

~JAMES 1:4 (KJV)

EIGHT: RESTING IN IT

Have you ever felt like God does a really good job of giving you a bomb preview to a movie? You start watching without realizing it's a preview because of its ability to captivate you. You completely forgot when you looked at the time stamp that shows how long the video is, that it only said five minutes, not five hours. And you get engulfed in the video, and you're like, "Oh my goodness! This is so good!" But then it abruptly stops, showing you the date, and "coming soon." And you're like, "What are you talking about, 'coming soon?' I was just all into this thing." Now you're frustrated because you're like, "Man, how could it be that it's not coming out yet? You let me get this excited about a preview?"

That's how it is with vulnerability. Sometimes, God will give you a preview and allow you to be in the moment, only to come and snatch it back, giving you the mandate to wait a certain number of days before the movie becomes available for you to watch. Many times, He does that because you are really not prepared to watch the entire movie at the time He allowed you to watch the preview. You would miss the message embedded in the movie that you were meant to see in the first place.

Nevertheless, you are frustrated because now you have to rest in it. And you're telling God, "I thought this season was mine to lay hold of certain things, but now you're saying it's not my season? What frustration! God, I've fasted, I've prayed, and I've done everything you asked. I even let go of everything that I knew was keeping me from you. I just knew that it was your design to give me everything that you had laid up for me."

Hear God saying, "But I didn't tell you that." God will come back and proclaim, "But there's still more. I found one other thing, one other blemish on you that I have got to get off. There's one more person's life that you need to impact before I can let you take off. They won't take off until you take off. You can't leave them too soon."

Consequently, I have found myself trying to reason with God. I thought it was written, it was now the time, and then something gets in the way. How many times do you thank God when something just comes up? Do you get so irritated with Him that things are not happening right now that you, as my mother often says, "Can't see the forest for the trees?"

Oftentimes, when you are vulnerable, dealing with matters of the heart and of purposeful pain at that, you find it scary to trust that there's something better out there. However, if you're a kingdom kid, you should already have those types of expectations. Paul says it like this in 1 Cor. 2:9: "But as it is written, Eye hath not seen, nor ear heard, neither have entered into the heart of man, the things which God hath prepared for them that love Him." (KJV)

Although you are fully aware of what the Word says, skepticism rears its ugly head. Life's lessons and life's pains can make you question: did God really say what He said? You don't want to go through the pain of incremental elevation. You want to be free, on purpose and for real this time, right away. When God is taking you up and down and round and round on this roller-coaster called life, your biggest concern is when will it all end. The toughest season to sit in with God is the one that you have to rest in, in God. And it's not easy because you see one thing happening, but it doesn't appear to be in alignment with what you believe God to be saying at this juncture.

I am reminded of the story of Noah, wherein God told him to prepare for this deluge of rain that was sure to come and flood a place that had never even experienced the dew of the morning, let alone rain of any magnitude. On top of that, Noah had to build this ark to God's specifications. Noah was 550 years old at the time that he covenanted with God to build the ark, which took fifty years to complete. Seven days after he finished building the ark, the rains came and the world as the people of Noah's day knew it would be no more. How many of us would endure fifty years of ridicule and derision, trying to do something that the natural man could never comprehend?

It is the nature of man to want to see God's promises fulfilled in a timely manner in accordance with your time clock. You must realize that God may change the process, but He never changes His plans for our lives. The hardest thing to do is to rest in it when you're not seeing God's promise come to fruition speedily.

How do you handle God's delay, which is not necessarily a denial? You remind God that He knows how hard you worked; He knows how much you gave. In fact, He knows how many parts of you had to die for you to become the woman who He is beholding right now. God says, "I know. I get that you're frustrated. I'm aware that a lot of you had to die to become who you are because I did the pruning. While a lot of you had to die, there's a lot more of you that has to come alive."

Dear reader, you know that Rome was not built in a day. Planting a seed does not yield an immediate harvest. Seedtime and harvest are not simultaneous. Everything happens in its season. And there is a reason for a season for everything. God may have planted lilies in you, but they will not bloom in December, so you will have to wait until April to enjoy the fragrance of your lilies in full bloom. If you could only realize that although you don't see the flowers in the winter months, that does not mean that the plant is dead. You must allow nature to take its course, for in due season you will reap a harvest if you do not become faint of heart.

Perhaps you should find comfort in the words of Jeremiah 29:11 that asserts: "'For I know the thoughts I think toward you,' declares the LORD, 'thoughts of peace, and not of evil, to give you a future and a hope.'" (NKJV) Remember, dear reader, as long as God, who knows the future, provides your agenda and goes with you as you fulfill His mission, you can have boundless hope.

May you endeavor to never run ahead of God. Sometimes you think you are ready to be in that marriage, in that relationship, or in that job or in this business, but only God knows what is on the other side. So, what I implore you to do is this: instead of saying, "God I'm ready for this," ask Him, "God, please prepare me for this."

The truth of the matter is, you don't know what's on the other side of the blessing. His promises are yea and amen. Yes, God's thoughts for you are to bring prosperity, but there are demons that come with prosperity. Can you handle them? Do you think that the enemy is going to stop fighting you and badgering you because the blessing showed up? No, he is going to come at you harder than ever because his design is to make you miscarry or abort God's plan for your life. The enemy (Satan) does not care what trimester you're in; he just does not want that baby to be birthed at all costs.

On the other side of the struggle, you find yourself changing the tides and shifting into the things of God. Now you say, "God prepare me for the blessing that you have prepared for me." You do know that in order to elevate with God, there is always a process. It is never just quick, fast, and easy.

VULNERABILITY

James 1:2-3 offers the steps to endurance: "My brethren, count it all joy when ye fall into divers temptations; knowing this, that the trying of your faith worketh patience." (KJV) It is important that we allow "...patience to have her perfect work, that ye may be perfect and entire, wanting nothing" (James 1:4 KJV).

In this next season, you don't want to be deprived of the very nutrients that you need to bloom in your garden. Please don't get frustrated in your resting season because that is a necessary and sensitive season wherein the enemy works his best to discourage you. He wants you to say, "I don't like what this feels like. I don't understand what this means. I don't like what this does, so I'm just going to do things my way."

If you ever want to miscarry a blessing that God has deposited in you to birth, just take matters into your own hands. Just begin to get an ego and say, "I can do this myself. I can do this in my own strength," and watch just how badly this turns out for you. My dears, there is nothing you can do in our own strength. That is why Proverbs 3: 5-6 admonishes: "Trust in the LORD with all thine heart; and lean not unto thine own understanding. In all thy ways acknowledge Him, and He will direct thy paths." (KJV)

You would do well to allow God to direct you because using your GPS does not work well. Most of us cannot read a roadmap, and others of us do not even listen to the GPS, even though it's yelling, "Turn left!" So, what about our way of thinking suggests to us that we have the ability to tell God what He should do in orchestrating our lives? We can't find our socks in the morning without divine intervention.

Dear readers, endeavor to rest in the resting season, learn in the resting season, and prep for the resting season. Any successful businessperson will tell you that they started preparing before the title came. If that were not the case, you can rest assured that they no longer hold that title or the business has folded because someone did not stop to count the cost.

LAUREN J.

If you are trying to be successful at anything worth having, you must exercise discipline and training, meaning there is a process that you must matriculate through. Rest in your process, knowing that God has not forgotten about you. His promises are sure! It does not matter how long it takes for your blessing to overtake you. God is trying to perfect you, but you're still agitated and trying to micromanage Him, as though that were possible. He is your Father. He is the One who is sovereign and in control of every design and every movement of man. Only God knows when to say, "Let there be," and things are brought into focus in your life. His designs turn into masterpieces that are beheld for ages to come, just as we do the masterpieces of Michelangelo.

But remember, there is a process. Trust the process and rest in it!

HE SAYS, "BE STILL, AND KNOW THAT I AM GOD..."

~PSALM 46:10 (KJV)

NINE: NOT REJECTED, BUT PROTECTED

On this journey of vulnerability, you often find yourself concerned about whether you're doing what God requires of you or you're yielding to the desires of your flesh. There appears to be a constant vacillation, going back and forth, because if you are truthful, you didn't want to be vulnerable in the first place. Now vulnerability is not an option, and all things must be done to the glory of God.

Sometimes the rejection is the very thing that brings God glory because He wants to see what will you choose when what He gives you doesn't look like what was promised. Will you choose to believe God, even when it doesn't look like what you know God said it is? Will you continue to choose God's word over your disappointment? When the enemy says, "This is not going to work out; you should have never opened up to them. They don't mean you any good," will you abort the mission when God has clearly told you there was purpose? That's what happens in the rejection season. Let's talk about it.

Oftentimes, rejection is literally God's protection of our lives. Every stumbling block, or every caution sign, or every detour does not mean that God has changed His mind about the promise. Sometimes it is necessary that you take a detour for your own safety. That way, you are not thrown off-track. It is all in how you interpret the detour that God sends. Satan would love to have you interpret it on this wise: "See, God wasn't going to come through anyway." Or, "You thought that was God, but was that really Him telling you to go and be and to show up in these places?"

Sure, it was. You go with the expectation of one thing, but God goes with the expectation of another. So, when you show up to the place where God has ordained and told you to just "be," sometimes He's only wanting you to show up to plant the seed, not to reap the harvest. But the problem that you have is that you are ready for God to do His work right now. God, I don't want to wait on harvest season. Although you just planted the seed, you're ready to eat right now.

How many of you understand that the day that you plant the seed is not the day you realize the harvest? There is a process involved, and God is in charge of the longevity of the process. Now, what you do on the sidelines is what determines if and when you will eat the fruit. During the growth process, manifold things take place. First of all, the rain comes but sometimes, you have to deal with other vagaries of the elements. Oftentimes, there is too much sunlight and not enough rain. Hail storms come and beat upon your tender vegetation which can stunt its growth. Then you have to go out there and make sure to pull out the weeds that have the potential of choking the life out of your plant. These things come to suffocate your purpose.

Suffocation comes in the form of negative people or negative thoughts that you tell yourself about yourself. Negativity will kill the seed before it actually undergoes the germination process wherein it dies in the Earth, only to live again. Then there is the fertilizer, the nasty thing that you have to throw on it, the dung that actually helps to sure it up. I call that your brokenness, the dissemination of your brokenness being heaped upon that seed. You have to find ways to shake it off, right? But then, there is a season where there is much needed rain—showers of blessings—that keeps the farmer inside as God is blessing the seed.

Consider this analogy as recorded in 1 Cor. 3:6-7: "I have planted, Apollos watered; but God gave the increase. So then neither is he that planteth anything, neither he that watereth; but God that giveth the increase." (KJV) Remember, man's extremity is God's opportunity. After you have done all that you know to do, then God will do what only He can do.

The Bible articulates the growth process in this fashion: "For the earth bringeth forth fruit of herself; first the blade, then the ear, after that the full corn in the ear." (Mark 4:28 KJV) All things are done according to God's perfect plan and timing. When the blade appears, that is a reminder of what that seed was when you originally planted it. What is beautiful about a seed is that the enemy doesn't have a clue about what it is until it starts to become. It's the same thing with people. No one knows what you have planted in your garden until it starts to evolve.

Some of you have what I call the greenhouse mentality. You want things that are force ripened, having been placed in a hot greenhouse that accelerates growth. You must remember that when something matures prematurely, it cannot withstand the storms of life. Bugs and animals will come along and devour what you have planted and nurtured that you did not allow to follow due course. It is the same with humans who hurry along the maturation process because you are seeking independence; you're not ready for the next level of attacks that are headed your way.

The enemy wants to destroy what you have worked so hard to preserve. See clearly, dear readers, that sometimes rejection is indeed God's protection. Hear Him saying, "No, don't come outside right now. The timing is all wrong. You're not ready." For many of you, if you come outside too early, you will become discouraged at what you experience and abort the mission. You'll stop coming for it, stop checking for it, and you will begin to plant seeds of discord and doubt that make you say, "I don't even want this anymore."

My dears, that is like music to the enemy's ear when you say, "I don't even want this anymore." He wants you to give up on the very thing that God has promised you because you look crazy going out there and saying, "I know there's a harvest coming," but you haven't seen it, yet. "I know my husband is coming, but I haven't seen him, yet. So, why don't I just date others?" God is saying, "No, you can't date others because your husband IS coming. I don't have time for you to go and fill your bucket with things that are not going to bring me glory."

Realize that doing things averse to God's leading will allow things to cut on you and leave you with scars. Have you ever had scar tissue and had to go through another surgical procedure to remove it? Scar tissue removal surgery lends itself to the potential of a vicious cycle of more surgeries. God doesn't want you to have to go through that. It is therefore important to understand that in the seasons in which you feel rejected, you are actually being protected by God. He loves you too much to allow you to hinder yourself. He loves you too much to let you come into a room that is not prepared to receive you.

Not every closed door is a locked door. On the other side of the closed door is someone who is still in preparation to receive you. Those who need to be around when you enter aren't there yet, and God loves them enough to not let them miss you, the blessing who is there to release them from the pain they're in. So, everything that God does, all of His timing, all of the ways that He moves with and in us, is so beautiful.

Sometimes He has to break your heart to get the lessons

out of you, so that you can go and impact and infiltrate the next generation. How can I talk to you about rejection unless I've been rejected? How can I talk to you about wanting to give up unless I've wanted to give up? Some things I've got to feel, so that I can impact you. Some things God has to train my mind about, so when it comes up for you, I can tell you how I did it. That's what vulnerability is all about—giving the most intimate parts of you to people when you don't really know what they're going to do with them. But you're okay with who you are, so much so, that it doesn't matter.

As you travel through vulnerability, may you become resolute to leave all things in God's hands. May you settle on the premise that God's rejection is part and parcel of His protection. He loves you too much to want you to fail, but is gracious enough to give you the option to choose.

"WAIT ON THE LORD; BE OF GOOD
COURAGE, AND HE SHALL STRENGTHEN
YOUR HEART; WAIT, I SAY, ON THE LORD!"

~PSALM 27:14 (NKJV)

TEN: LORD, I DON'T KNOW

Through this process, I have had moments where I felt like I was extremely clear about God's direction for my life. Yes, it was very clear what He wanted me to do concerning my vulnerability. I was really feeling God's pulse concerning my letting others in. But how many times have you felt, "I know now exactly what I should be doing," and just like that, God puts a completely different plan in place? The next thing you know, you're like, "I thought I had it, but I honestly don't know what is going on."

That is exactly the season I sit in. Some days, I think I've got it figured out, and I think, "Oh my goodness God, I know exactly what you're wanting. I'm seeing the manifestation and I'm seeing the big picture. The blueprint has been downloaded in my spirit, and all I have to do is follow it." Then God throws in an "I don't know" moment.

In this season of uncertainty, I don't know where I belong or whom I belong to. I almost feel like, as weird as this thing might sound, a house dog! I got out of the gate because it looked like it would be more fun on the outside.

43

VULNERABILITY

I found a way to sneak out, and I took it. Now, I'm out in the world, and it doesn't look nearly as great as it did when I was behind the gate.

Things are not always what they seem. I find myself wondering, "Should I have left my comfort zone to explore uncharted waters that seemed to be calm and inviting only to experience turbulence on the other side?" I know greater is coming based on the promises of God, but did I leave Jerusalem too quickly, so to speak? At least I knew I would get a couple of meals, shelter, and my bills paid. Now I'm out here wondering where my next meal is going to come from. I sleep, but I don't rest. I'm very uneasy about whom God is really calling me to be and do. At first, I was cool with whom I thought He was calling me to be, but now, not so much.

I am pretty sure that as you read this book you can attest to having felt the chill of uncertainty at some point in your life. You, too, may be saying, "God I followed you because I felt as though I understood your will and plan for my life, but now I'm out here and I really don't know."

My dears, there is absolutely nothing comfortable about walking with God. I don't know who said that walking with Him was going to allow you to breathe a sigh of relief. The truth of the matter is, walking with God affords you anxiety at best. One of your human attributes is that you want to know exactly what is expected of you, and you want that sense of belonging. It is so important in relationships that your partner knows that they belong in your world. They belong in your heart, dreams, and goals. The worst situation I can imagine is being with a person and never feeling at home in their orbit. And when you're in a season with God, and you can say, "I don't know if I even belong in this. Did I miss God altogether?", that's how I feel.

I was sharing with a girlfriend/mentor, and I said to her, "When I was married, I knew exactly what was expected of me." In retrospect, I felt like I had a good grasp on what I was doing and why I was doing it. I even knew how long I would be doing it. I felt like I really knew my job and my role as a wife, businesswoman, and mother. Then I got knocked completely off the ledge in *Purposeful Pain*, and now I am climbing back up the ladder, a different ladder altogether.

Now it's a little tricky because the previous ladder that I was on didn't have all of these steps. The steps are farther apart, requiring more stretching on my part to continue to ascend to the top. I question God about why the stretches are longer and the strides farther than are comfortable. Really, I didn't sign up for this ladder! I find myself craving the familiar. I can identify with the children of Israel when they journeyed from Egypt to the Promised Land and were met with adversity. Although God was leading them, providing them with sustenance in the form of manna from heaven, guiding them as a pillar of cloud by day and a pillar of fire by night, they were ready for what had been promised but didn't like the process.

So, here I am, out here with God, and I'm gung-ho about the promise, about what it's going to produce. But in the same breath I'm thinking, "I'm sure that I never signed up for all of this, though." I'm of the opinion that I'm strong enough to do everything God is requiring of me because if I wasn't, I would never have been afforded the opportunity. But I'm also concerned that I don't know if I want it as badly as God wants it for me.

Vulnerability is one of those things that takes you out of your element. There is nothing you can do in preparation for it. My thoughts are such that I don't know what God wants from me. I don't know what His plans are for my life. I understand that the promise will always outlive the pain, but there are times when I question whether I'm going to make it to the other side. How much longer is the process going to take before I realize the prize? I hear God saying, "Just keep walking. This requires a forward motion." Every day you wake up brings you closer to "The" day. I'm like, "Lord, just help me to make it to 'The' day because my faith is starting to wane."

VULNERABILITY

Dear readers, just know that you are not alone. I, too, swim in that sea of uncertainty. Just because you have come to the resolve that God's will and God's way is the only place of safety, doesn't mean that you know the path or even the terrain upon which you are called to embark. God never shows His hand from the outset because He knows we'll either abort the plan or miscarry it by interjecting our finite thinking. He loves us so much that He would rather hurt our feelings than crush our hearts.

God allows you incremental elevation coupled with incremental instructions, lest you dash your hopes and circumvent your expected end. Because God doesn't let you in on what awaits you at the end of the journey, you feel isolated. You begin to grumble because God is not showing you enough. How can you partner with Him when He won't let you in on the minute details of the plan? All the while God is saying, "You can't handle more."

My dears, you must trust that God's way, timing, and process is perfectly tailored just for you. So, I urge you to stay on the ride. Don't abandon your place of safety. Consider this: It's a good thing to have a boat on the water, but it's a grave hour when the water gets in the boat. Don't poke a hole in your purpose by trying to go ahead of God. Only God can see into the future. Only God can see all the pitfalls along the way. It is given to you to walk by faith each day. Soon it will all be over.

Allow me to share this: I had a season where I truly believed I had met the man who was heaven-sent just for me. But in the fourth quarter of my season, God pulled out a star player who was red-shirted. He pulled out a player whom I wasn't expecting to join the game. God called for a substitution, and that made me sit back and say, "Wait God, was this the plan? Was this your move all along?" Listen, I didn't see that coming. I wasn't prepared for that, and now I just don't know. I felt secure getting to know this one guy, but then God pulls a switcheroo!

That is one of the things that will trouble new believers

or those in a new relationship, especially if you're relying on God's guidance. Be ready for detours and possible layovers along the way to your destiny. As a human, you want to know what is expected of you, where you are headed, what the journey will look like, and how you will know when you've arrived. Just like being in a relationship, you want to know that when you turn your back to your mate to slip away into dreamland, you can rest assured that your partner only has eyes for you and that they have your best interest at heart at all times.

It's the same thing with God. You want the assurance that God is with you on this trek through the wilderness of life. No matter what mistakes you might make along the way, you need to know that God will not abandon you. Your human side is of the logic that if you do certain things that are averse to God's will for your life, He will push away from you. Satan would have you believe that God is with you only as long as you follow His mandates. Truthfully, God is with you whether you're doing what He wants or not. It is all in how you see it. It's still a very tough situation to be in, having to say, "God, I just don't know."

Consequently, as I continue to try to take it slow, being an alpha female, allowing God to do His perfect work in me requires a greater level of trust. It is an everyday process. You don't just wake up one morning having complete trust in God. It requires a level of comfort on your part. My plea is for grace to trust Him more. I am ready for Him to just manifest His power and bring to full fruition His perfect plan for my life. Bring into focus the prize or the perfect gift that He's been grooming me for. Lay out the plan in its totality, God. I believe I'm ready to walk in it. Pray for me, dear readers, as I continue to rest in, "Lord, I don't know."

"FOR WHO HAS KNOWN THE MIND OF THE LORD, SO AS TO INSTRUCT HIM?"

~1 COR. 2:16 (NIV)

ELEVEN: DON'T GET OFF THE RIDE BEFORE IT STARTS

I've had to remind myself of this very thing the entire time that I've been writing this treatise: "Don't get off the ride before it starts!" Have you ever walked up to a roller-coaster that someone talked you into riding, and you knew that you did not want to ride? Yet you allowed someone to influence you to go ahead and get on the ride. So here you go, giving yourself this pep talk all the way leading up to mounting the ride. "This ride can't defeat me, although I know I am afraid of heights. It will be over soon. I know I can get through this." You're prepping yourself the entire time because you know that your gut is asking you, "What's going on? Why are you getting on this ride? You know you don't want to do this." Besides that, you're watching people as they're on the ride. Some seem to be enjoying it, while others are screaming frantically to make it stop. Some may even be contemplating jumping off in midair. You know in your heart of hearts that once you get on, you will be wishing you never did. But for whatever reason you get on anyway. The entire time the ride is inching up, you're trying to figure out why?

The ride begins to move, making the little "shoo" sound that it makes as it's inching along, and you know now that you can't get off. That's the moment that I sit in. The moment when the ride has just started to take off and there's that small window of opportunity where you could scream, "Stop! Let me off!" but you don't. You just sit there. And, as it goes up and up and up, you hear that clanking noise underneath your butt, the slow grinding noise, and you begin to realize this was the stupidest idea ever! Then you turn and look back and see how far you are from the starting point, and you realize there's no turning back. In fact, there is no reverse mode on the ride, just a forward thrust until you're back safely on the ground. So, you say, "God, I'm going to make the best of this, but if you get me off, I'm never getting on again."

I am almost certain that you have felt this way before about a relationship or about getting on a ride, period. Perhaps a situation or a career move has made you feel this way, and you're trying to decide whether this was a good move or not. It's amazing because of course, the entire time, you're just sitting there thinking, "Why did I embark on this journey?"

Yes, that's where I sit. I'm on this vulnerability roller-coaster thinking, "Why did I even influence others to get on with me?" What's worse is when you get on the ride and you want to get off but you can't because it was your idea in the first place. It was because of you and your big mouth that others bought into the plan. It was you who sold them on the idea of how great this would be. Now you've started thinking, "It's really not that great, and I want to get off." That's me, Lauren J., the woman who was the catalyst for a following of men and women looking to hitch their wagons to a star and soar to higher heights. That equates to them hopping on the vulnerability train with me, anticipating a wild but successful ride, when all the while I'm wanting to abort. God whispers, "Don't get off before the ride takes off."

Many a time, you ask God for things that you believe you are prepared for, but the truth is, you're really not. I think the worst thing that can happen to you is when God gives you your blessing too early because you are frustrated and begin to press Him to give you your portion. You are ready to give up midstream, but God is taking His time. He's not coming within the time frame that you set for yourself. That is the most daunting situation to be in. Your unwillingness to wait on the Lord and be of good courage could cause you to miss Him altogether.

The consequences of being hasty are equal to the rude awakening that, had you been willing to wait another thirty seconds, the breakthrough would be within your grasp. Had you waited thirty seconds, thirty being the number of maturity, the relationship you had been begging God for would be about to manifest in your life. Perhaps God had to ready him for you and you for him. You had been on the potter's wheel and are now ripe for the taking, but the man you desire needed a little more work. Your patience ran out. You were scared because you didn't know what this thing was about to look like.

As I take inventory of my life, there were moments when I sabotaged God's will because I was unwilling and fearful of waiting. Perhaps dear readers, that's you or that has been you. Truly waiting on the prize can be more frightening than the actual manifestation. The idea of waiting too long is tantamount in your mind, causing you to miss the lesson on what to do while you wait. We major in the minor and minor in the major. We miss the message as recorded in Isaiah 40:30-31 that states, *"But they that wait upon the LORD shall renew their strength; they shall mount up with wings as eagles; they shall run, and not be weary; and they shall walk, and not faint."*

LAUREN J.

(KJV) That screams in my spirit, "Don't get off the ride before it starts! You have been safely locked in!"

> "AND JESUS SAID UNTO HIM, 'NO MAN,
> HAVING PUT HIS HAND TO THE PLOUGH,
> AND LOOKING BACK, IS FIT FOR THE
> KINGDOM OF GOD.'"
>
> ~LUKE 9:62 (KJV)

TWELVE: SHOT CLOCK

You're in the fourth quarter of a situation, and the shot clock is winding down. Should you take the shot hastily before the buzzer goes off, even though you're not in position? This chapter is about understanding that although you're in the last hour of this thing, the last few seconds, you don't have to shoot aimlessly without contemplation.

You've heard various quotes concerning time, such as, "Time waits for no one." And perhaps you've even said, "I don't have time for this." As a human, you likely really struggle with time management. When you mismanage your time, you fall in the predicament of rushing against the shot clock. How many times have you rushed into a relationship, rushed into a situation, rushed into a job, rushed into a friendship that God had not ordained for you? Perhaps there have been relationships that God has called on you to impact but not stay in. If you stop to examine the fourth quarter of the game of life, you'll likely find that you've done nothing productive with the time you were given to grow and to build, to evolve and to elevate. At best, you grossly squandered precious time. You become frustrated because God is taking too long, and in the last ten seconds, you make hasty moves when you should be making the most calculated move that you've made all game.

The funniest thing about the shot clock is that it is designed to alert you as to how close you are to the end, but not to make you rush to get there. And I'll be honest; I've been guilty in this season of vulnerability of thinking, "God, I'm gonna miss my time to shoot my shot and score."

But how many of you realize there's no missing a shot when you're walking with God? The beauty of God and of having Him in the forefront of our existence is that He doesn't operate in time. He is the great orchestrator of it. He lives in the future of our lives, as well as the present and the past. He is the only one who knows the end of a thing even before it commences. God is always there to ensure that we make it on time, even when it seems that time has run out. I'm reminded of a narrative recorded in Joshua 10:12-14 where at Joshua's request, God caused the sun to stand still for several hours, so that Israel could achieve a greater victory over her enemy. This was one of two times in the Old Testament of the Holy Writ when God interrupted the celestial clock as a sign to a man. The other occasion was when God turned back the sundial ten points for the benefit of Hezekiah in Isaiah 38: 7-8. God will move heaven and earth for His children who are willing to wait on Him.

My dears, you rush so quickly, not paying attention to all of the lessons to be gleaned when God quiets you. God is resolute to crush out of you those things that are not like Him in order to ready you for the next level. If you are not patient as God does His perfect work in you, you end up in situations uncrushed, still needing pruning. So, you mishandle and eventually watch the demise of a relationship, a friendship, or a career, all because you saw the shot clock and thought, "Let me hurry up and shoot my shot."

VULNERABILITY

The beauty of the process is that you should never be so anxious to shoot that you miss the dynamics of what it takes to get prepared to score. Let's talk basketball. Basketball has a lot to do with form and a lot to do with how you hold your arms when you prepare to shoot. It is more about form and process than the act of shooting at the basket. The idea is that if you can master the form, when you attempt your shot, there is a greater chance that you'll score.

Sometimes, you don't want to take the time to get in the proper position, and you just wing it. You don't want to dribble the ball down the court, set up the play, and pass the ball to the player in the best position to take the shot. You want to throw the ball from the other end of the court, hoping it will miraculously find the goal and not just bounce off of the rim.

The thing about being with God is that He is more concerned about your posture than you scoring because He said that your expected end was predetermined by Him. This means you don't have to wait until the game is over to shout because you know in the end you always win with God on your side. God already knows that many of you will become overwhelmed by the process of training. He knows that you have the propensity to become frustrated, lackadaisical, and inconsistent in your quest to work through the details. But also with many of us, God knows that you're going to practice your form every single day until you obsess over getting it right. Still, some of you will get out on the court with no training, no practice, and just throw the ball in the direction of the basket on a wing and a prayer. Don't be anxious because the clock is winding down. With God as your Life Coach, you're on the winning team. Trust the process; it is designed to groom and grow you.

God sends people into your life for a reason and a season. Some people are only for such a time as this. While others are only pivots in your travels, some are for a lifetime. But you will never truly know which slot a person fits in if you never go through the process of pruning and watching character. Some of you are guilty of hopping into relationships because you are tired. You believe that you have waited long enough. "God, I've given enough. God, I've been celibate." Yes, you have done all of this stuff to align yourself, but was it just so you could shoot your shot? Are you mastering the process as to form?

When you are only focused on being able to position yourself for making the score, you will miss out on all the great lessons that will propel you and sustain you in the forming season. I don't want you to miss your form. That's the beauty of preparing to score. The clock is there to reassure you that there will be a time that this too shall end, but it is not there to make you rush to end it more quickly than God has designed. You often misconstrue what the timer is really there for. Don't rush into this next season because you're so anxious to be done with the process. I know you're ready to take the shot and to know who has won the game. You just want to head to the locker room, get your Gatorade fix, hear your coach's parting words and hurry yourself home to rest. How many of you know that there is no true rest when you are working with God? He gives us a reprieve, but there is always another mountain to climb.

That's the thing about seasons: you're either in one, about to get into one, or on your way out. Learn to embrace whatever season God has you in. Don't get so consumed with making sure that you shoot your shot to score. But know this, as long as your form is correct, when it is time for you to prepare for your last shot, your form will make sure that you score. You won't miss out. That marriage, that spouse, that mate that God has for you will be yours if you learn to wait.

The reason He seems to be slow in coming to your aid is because you have mishandled your time. God knows that if He throws you the ball and you have not taken the time to make sure that your feet are properly settled, your arms are properly extended, and that bend in your knees is just right to form the posture for the perfect shot, you will quickly just shoot. There is a lot to be said about training for this moment of scoring.

Have you been coming and putting in the practice and the work, making the requisite preparation, so that when the game begins, you are physically fit and mentally ready for the long haul? Are you just praying that you get in the game so that you can shoot, using a form that you concoct on the spot? Are you content to just fake it until you make it? I'd rather see you "faith" it until you make it. Always be prepared for a thing rather than just show up to a thing because you never know what you'll be up against. God gives you time for proper preparation, but do you use it wisely? More often than not, you waste time and time that is wasted can never be recovered.

My dears, when you're in the wee hours and the clock is ticking, don't just throw the ball in the direction of the goal to see if you'll make it. That type of resolve is akin to taking a shot in the dark. The result is that you're irritated, aggravated, and frustrated with God because He didn't do the miraculous when you, in all honestly, settled for the status quo. It is in the forming season that God takes you and wrings you like a wet towel, getting all of the water out until you are ready to be formed.

I can promise you that forming is that time in the vulnerability season where you have to get really comfortable with your uncomfortable truth. This is designed to ready you for taking a profitable shot. And for women, that is a hard concept because you want to hurry up and be loved. You want to hurry up and wake up in your lover's arms. You long to love and have it be reciprocated. You don't want to wait on your lover to form. Truth is, many of you are hurting and you are just ready to find refuge. You've been traveling, and you're tired; you just want to lay your weary head on your lover's chest and hear a heart beating just for you. In light of the shot clock, this is not a season of rest and repose. It's time to form up, get in the proper position, and score. Don't miss your shot trying to shoot against the clock!

> *"FOR EVERYTHING THERE IS A SEASON AND*
> *A TIME FOR EVERY PURPOSE UNDER*
> *HEAVEN..."*
>
> *~ECCLESIASTES 3:1 (ASV)*

THIRTEEN: AT LAST...

D
o you ever wonder when will you reach the destiny of "At Last?" Have you ever pondered how far away are you from being able to finally reach the pivotal point of laying down your heart's baggage and breathing a sigh of relief? You long for the assurance that this time it's real, and you no longer have to worry about abandonment, disappointment, or worse, repairing your heart after the love that was supposedly yours walked away.

What if I told you that "At Last" wasn't a happy ending with a vacation on a remote island with the love of your life, but actually a lifetime of finally accepting your flaws, embracing your growth, and accepting your truth?

When I first started this journey of "Vulnerability," I dreamed of it being my documented journey to meeting my purpose mate. Somewhere during the season in which I wrote this chapter, I thought that I had found the safest place on earth in a King that was designed for me. To my surprise, I found a King, but in finding him, I learned to accept me. So, as I romanticized the idea of falling in love with a person who had the capacity to love all of my flaws and be able to celebrate my successes, I ultimately found all of that in me.

Sometimes the "At Last" is not about finding love but about finally falling in love with yourself. The hardest part about unraveling my life's journey was having to hear myself relive those moments. Rehearsing the highs, remembering the lows, and daydreaming about what the future could hold after taking a two-year journey, only to discover that finally fully loving me was the "At Last" that I could never outlast.

Accepting myself was me accepting my anointing, walking boldly in my God-given gifts, forgiving myself for giving myself to people who never desired to value me, and lastly, accepting words as confirmation, not validation. There is a certain power that you take hold of when you realize that the "At Last" you had been waiting on all of this time was just the authentic version of you...AT LAST!

*"TO ACQUIRE WISDOM IS TO LOVE
ONESELF; PEOPLE WHO CHERISH
UNDERSTANDING WILL PROSPER."
~PROVERBS 19:8 (NLT)*

ABOUT THE AUTHOR

*L*AUREN GRIMES-JACKSON, *is the Amazon Best-Selling author of* Purposeful Pain, *the highly anticipated blog turned E-book* Intimacy, *and her newest release,* Vulnerability: The Art of Letting Go. *She is also the app owner of "The Purpose", which is available in both iTunes and Google play.*

Lauren was born and reared in Opelousas, LA. She is first and foremost a Christian woman whose life is dedicated to helping bridge healthy relationships between women and men, through her own life experiences, and journey toward wholeness.

Lauren obtained a Bachelor of Science degree from Northwestern State University, in Natchitoches, LA, a Master of Science Degree in Banking and Financial Management, and also a

M.B.A. both from New England College in Henniker, NH.

Lauren's aspiration is to promote healing and liberation from the perpetual cycle of brokenness often associated with the vagaries of life. Lauren acclaims herself as being the bridge to helping men and women merge their passion into their God-designed purpose. She is a certified life coach, with years of experience in corporate coaching.

Lauren enjoys public speaking and sharing her knowledge about becoming an author, branding, and finance. She has been a speaker for women's conferences, the Shreveport-Bossier African American Minority Expo, and a panelist speaker for the Shreveport/Bossier Ladies in Leadership luncheon. In 2019, Lauren was an honoree for the Athena Award, and she was also a part of the 2019 40 under 40 Class, both hosted by the local chamber.

Lauren currently resides in Shreveport, LA, and is a proud mother of two handsome boys. She is also a successful entrepreneur in the arena of mortgage lending. Lauren is a Mortgage Loan Officer for Planet Home Lending Mortgage Company and has been in the banking industry for over ten years.

Made in the USA
Monee, IL
19 July 2021